DURING

ALSO BY JAMES RICHARDSON

JAMES RICHARDSON DURING

COPPER CANYON PRESS

PORT TOWNSEND, WASHINGTON

Printed in the United States of America

Cover art: Erika Blumenfeld, *Light Recording: August Full Moon* (detail), 2004. Chromogenic print, aluminum panel, laminate. 48 x 85 inches. www.erikablumenfeld.com

Copper Canyon Press is in residence at Fort Worden State Park in Port Townsend, Washington, under the auspices of Centrum. Centrum is a gathering place for artists and creative thinkers from around the world, students of all ages and backgrounds, and audiences seeking extraordinary cultural enrichment.

LIBRARY OF CONGRESS CATALOGING-IN-PUBLICATION DATA
Richardson, James, 1950–
  During / James Richardson.
    pages ; cm
  ISBN 978-1-55659-433-5 (pb : alk. paper)
  I. Title.

PS3568.I3178D87 2016
813'.54—dc23

2015015942
98765432 FIRST PRINTING

COPPER CANYON PRESS
Post Office Box 271
Port Townsend, Washington 98368
www.coppercanyonpress.org

ACKNOWLEDGMENTS

Some of these poems first appeared elsewhere:

Academy of American Poets: "Metamorphosis" was in the Poem-a-Day series.

Copper Nickel: "Vectors 4.3: A Summer Morning"

Hotel Amerika: About forty of the pieces in "Vectors" 4.1, 4.2, 4.3, and 4.4 were first published in the 2011 aphorism issue and reprinted in *The Pushcart Prize Anthology XXXVIII*.

Narrative: "Fourteen," "Quasar," "Solo," "Theory of Everything," "Vectors 4.4: One or Two Thoughts," "Very Late"

The Nation: "Notes for a Translation of an Ancient Fragment," "To the Next Centuries"

The New Yorker: "Big Scenes," "Essay on Clouds," "Essay on Wood"

Plume: "Vectors 4.1: A Few Thoughts in the Dark," "Vectors 4.2: Everyone Else"

Plume Anthology of Poetry 2013: "Antelope," "Essay on No"

T: The New York Times Style Magazine: "One of the Evenings"

Yale Review: "All the Right Tools," "Essay Traversed by Deer," "Late Aubade," "Watch"

A version of "Invasive Species" printed by David Sellers (as "Early and Late") was Princeton University's 2014 Phi Beta Kappa poem.

*

My happiest and deepest literary debts are to Connie Hassett, my cothinker and first, last, and best reader, and Cat Richardson, my favorite poet.

Particular thanks to David Orr, Sarah Manguso, and my twin, Renée Ashley, for reading the whole thing, and to Rob McQuilkin, whose sharp, volunteer assessment saved me a whole lot of internal debate.

And warm thanks to some poet-friends who maybe read a little, and certainly helped a lot, whether they knew it or not: Julie Agoos, Lily Akerman, Raf Allison, Judy Baumel, Dana Isokawa, Troy Jollimore, Meredith Martin, Sandy McClatchy, Paul Muldoon, Jeff Nunokawa, Maxine Patroni, Starry Schor, Brenda Shaughnessy, Tracy Smith, Lizzy Straus, Craig Teicher, Chase Twichell, Susan Wheeler, and C.K. Williams.

This manuscript was completed with the assistance of a 2013 Literature Fellowship from the National Endowment for the Arts.

ART WORKS.

National
Endowment
for the Arts
arts.gov

For Melinda and all the Mulls: Pete, Charley, Lucy,
Dave, Steve, Tom, Jennie

CONTENTS

Alternate Routes

Long Stories Short

Early and Late

DURING

To the Next Centuries

Is there autumn there, is there leaf smoke, is the air
blued and mapled, oaked and appled and wined,
is that tang, that ache for *who knows?*
gone from your sweaters and hair?
Are there trees, even, do they break out
in uncontrollable cold fires,
do they shatter in long, unreal downstreamings,
is October the same without them, is our sadness
so river-and-wind swift and so free, is it still
our sharpest seeing, if we have not learned from them
how to be taken apart, how to be blown away?

Are clouds the same, are they still our clouds
if leaves have never seethed against them
on a tempestuous night, are they wild, is the moon the same
if it has never wildly sailed through wild clouds,
is there a Hunter's Moon, a Blood Moon tinged
with the rust and incandescence of the leaves,
is there a moon at all, a hanging stone,
a white astonishment, the exile's breath on a pane?

There is sun, I am sure—has it grown more dangerous,
has its shine through thin ozone whited out your eyes,
does it drive dunes through your forests, has it warmed
the seas to exactly body temperature?
What is it like to have won and won and won,
no mile without its grid of roads,
no block unwired, no hand's width without wireless,
when every breeze has been rebreathed
each current steered, each cliff a mirror?

And what has endangered my imagination
that imagines you pale and bodiless and scanned,
not a shadow left in your floodlit brains,
sleep hard in coming, dreams shallow and bright?
Why do I see you in a white room drifting
among machines and drips and feeds
as if you were my dead, who went before me
on white boats launched into the future,

as if you were me, when I am tired,
as I am tired now, tired of the expertise
that says there is nothing new,
no thoughts or feelings not already words,
no words I have not said again and again,
thinking how long this trip has been, so near its end
that I will never again send down new roots,
change jobs, raise children, fall in love.
I can lighten my suitcase now, discarding my ticket,
since there is no return, the map of the city
I'll never get back to, the little blue phrase book
for the language I'll never speak, the sweater,
the half-read novel, the comb, the end of this thought...

I know you will never hear the squeak of a mailbox,
church bells (already quaint here), a van
graveling around a turn, a CD (surely gone).
(I won't ask—couldn't endure to know—are there birds there
still building the dawn.) I know you will never hear
this wind I'm hearing though there will be winds, the song
that's blowing me away, though there will be song
after song. You won't hear this, though you, like me,
will lose what seems like everything and go on, will cry
against your weariness with leaves and moon and wind,

or whatever passes then for moon and leaves and wind,
cry out against death and the dead world,
the dead world, and the death in you, until, like me,
you can stand again unborn, unused, unknown.

A Few Thoughts in the Dark

Again

Is Memory,
as they pretend,
mother of the Muse?—
or Forgetting,
who says *My friend,*
I know
you've told me before
about love, death,
solitude—and what
were those other things?—but
tell me again.

One of the Evenings

After so many years, we know them.
This is one of the older Evenings: its patience,
settling in, its warmth that needs nothing in return.
So many Augusts sitting out through sunset,
first a dimness in the undergrowth like smoke,
and then like someone you hadn't noticed
has been watching a long time…

It has seen everything that can be done in the dark.
It has seen two rifles swing around
to train on each other, it has seen lovers meet and revolve,
it has seen the wounds grayscale in low light.
It has come equally for those who prayed for it
and those who switched on lamp after lamp
until they could not see. It deals evenhandedly
with the one skimming the stairs as rapidly as typing,
the one washing plates a little too loudly,
the one who thinks there is something more important,
since it does not believe in protagonists,
since it knows anyone could be anyone else.

It has heard what they said aloud to the moon, to the stars
and what they could not say,
walking alone and together. It has gotten over
I cannot live through this, it has gotten over *This did not have to happen*
and *This is experience one day I will be glad for.*
It has gotten over *How even for a moment
could I have forgotten?* though it never forgets,
leaves nothing behind, does not believe in stories,
since nothing is over, only beginning somewhere else.

It could be anywhere but it is here
with the kids who play softball endlessly not keeping score,
though it's getting late, way too late,
holding their drives in the air like invisible moons a little longer,
giving way before them so they feel like they're running faster.
It likes trees, I think. It likes summer. It seems comfortable with us,
though it is here to help us be less ourselves.
It thinks of its darkening as listening harder and harder.

Essay Traversed by Deer

Only when met
by a bullet or an SUV
do they take on mass. Otherwise deer
are lighter than the paper
they sound like, skimming unshattered myrtle,
and die lightly of themselves,
spreading like sighs over weeks and acres:
a leaf-strewn pool
imperceptibly more tannic,
sunset brown each day a little earlier.

*

I forget and remember and forget
that they are bodily. Mornings, they are old cars
snorting and shuddering, moving badly in the cold,
but later in currents over unstirred leaves
they are shadows
of something else, and cast no shadows.

*

Try on the pain: Actaeon,
changed by Artemis,
extruding shins and hooves
and, white from his temples,

strange nudity of horns.
How he ran but could not
run past himself, outspeed
the arrows' hiss-straight heat,

and deep in the body of a deer,
its two small windows
too high to see out,
heard his friends' shouts

as he toppled,
and his own dogs bent to drink him.

*

Where a deer thinned quietly
and disassembled: heap of twigs.

*

When they split the deer lengthwise
and gut them, when they lay out for the dogs
the liver, and bread soaked in blood,
we are to remember the lips
of Sir Gawain brushing his lady's lips.

They lay out the liver, and soaked bread, and the *lights,*
which are the lungs because, riddled with air,
they will float, and also because a body
is what it feels, and I remember
in a long summer valley
breathing sunlight and pine
they won't find when they cut me open,
and my soles are the soft paths there,
and my eyes are sky, the sky my eyes.

*

I don't believe the mind is separate from the body,
which means: my mind
says it doesn't think it is.
Though the mind talks too much
and says stuff it doesn't believe.
Shut up, the body would say,
if it were the mind, *the Body*
is one of your stupid abstractions.
And the mind would get steamed
and go out for a walk, or rather
it would ride like a bubble the slow stream of the body
and think *I'm free, I'm free.*

*

Not sure the mind of a deer is anything
but speed and blurring trees and wind.

Their scat:
blueberries, coffee beans.

*

Poor creature of distance,
the mind is always on the wrong side
of its skin, of a word, of a window,
and tries to forget its isolation
in some ravishing, murmurous
rhythmriverwind (there it goes again,
and the body rolls its eyes...).

*

And sometimes, hearing us through glass,
though far
down the slope, they stiffen, scatter.

*

For the body, it is like being in the basement,
hearing the shrill of water turning on,
the groan of chairs slid out from the table,
the lightless thunder

of suddenly deliberate steps—
maybe the high gods, convened in judgment,
voting and going their ways—

or what the dead in the underworld
hear of what we go on doing,

the garrulous brain above it dimly
like a radio, or someone leaving a message
in the tone of not looking
in anyone's eyes, just talking, talking, talking.

*

And sometimes, hearing
nothing at all,

the deer
freeze,

so still they feel
deeply the soft

drills of stars.

Vectors 4.1: A Few Thoughts in the Dark

Let there be light. Had he awakened, confused about where he was? Had he been sitting on a stone a long time, not quite realizing how dark it had gotten?

*

The stars don't know which constellation they're in.

*

Night is of the Earth. The Sun goes away, and a darkness rises that was there all the time.

*

You need a thin film of dust and a surface it can slide on, say the bare floor under the bed. Watch a long time, and here a draft or there the soft concussions of your breath will compress the dust along a front. Watch longer, and these lines themselves collide, compressing further. That's how dust balls form or, on a larger scale, stars—moved, who knows, by the little winds of a sleeper turning on a mattress, or the cold fusions of his dreams.

*

What the dust calls will is wind.

*

Difficult to imagine an eternal *yes* vigilant enough to keep every closet and drawer of the universe this sharply in focus. Easier to feel someone is just forgetting to say *no*.

*

Bless the things so small there is no need to doubt them.

*

I can't remember a thing about my little brother's funeral except the tie I wore, still way back in my closet forty years later. I dare not throw it away, but I won't look at it because it's not black anymore but transparent like the night. Deep, deep in it there are very faint stars, and I'm afraid of what will happen if I stare long enough for them to come into focus.

*

On a winter night the stars are colder than the dark.

*

In the smallest hour I can hear it, the faint hiss I know is the tape of my life, but is it recording or playing?

*

What's the name for the color of leaves at night, a black you can't help seeing as green?

Solo

I was just trying to think where I was
on June 25, 1961:
Garden City, New York, certainly,
on Sunday, the worst day of the week,
when just nineteen miles away in Manhattan,
according to the sign on Stewart Avenue,
forty minutes by train and ten by subway,
Bill Evans's great, quiet solo on "Detour Ahead,"
was walking out on unbelievably thin ice,

so close, those Cold War kill-zone diagrams
in *Time* told us, that if they dropped
the Big One on Manhattan
in the future that hasn't yet happened
we'd had it—flash, shockwave, fallout.
The seventh grade debate was going to be
Should we all build backyard shelters?
and I was eleven. No mystery, then,

that my thoughts were elsewhere and I didn't hear him.
But what about yesterday? This same cut played
in this very study, the difference
between who I was and am
less than paper thin, and inflamed
by who knows what, I only half heard
and it didn't do a thing for me—
much less blow me away as it does

now, on January 23, 2013,
which would have been the sixtieth birthday
of my little brother, who has lived for decades

only in a universe divided from ours
by a thin wall I hear voices through,
tones more than words, something like laughter
that I want to be his (or is it
music I've left on, not sure where...).

It's hard to tell the faint laughter,
mostly women, who are harder to erase
(it's live at the Vanguard),
from the ice in the glasses—
excitement, coolness, delight—
even if they're not quite listening,
as Evans knew, thinking how life
is all the more moving for what,
if only for a minute, it can cease
to feel, and now he sends
his not knowing if anyone's there at all

back into his solo, persuading us
note by note it's better that way, the hurt music
listening more carefully to itself, and caring
all the more because tomorrow
even he might not. Though ages later
someone looks up from reading, hearing at last
This was for you. No, this made you, for seven minutes,
the one who was waiting only for this.

LaFaro, the bassist, liner notes tell you,
died in a car crash ten days later.
In a few years, John, our parents, friends
it's an indignity to number, and, who knows,
maybe some fireball at the speed of sound
is rushing back to us from a future
separated from now by a membrane

no thicker than the wall of my study (which it seems
my lamp is warming) to touch us all into nothing,

but still in 1961, knowing it's going to be
tomorrow and yesterday and today again
and again unpredictably,
and not even needing to think how difficult,
how difficult and beautiful it is, whatever in us weeps
because no one is weeping, and then laughs
because no one is laughing,

Evans is lifting, for anyone listening,
any weight they need to have lifted—no,
is making it weightless, note by note
cutting the tiny moorings
of something titanic in us that is straining
to rise and grow bright on what is still, for me,
January 23, 2013, though it's getting very late.

Sentence

So that's why prayers don't work: God doesn't speak English,
doesn't speak anything. His books are translations
from something not language, since to begin a sentence
is to drive from glare into the dimness of a tunnel,
losing the view of the harbor, the skyline, the heavens
(the universe of all you've left unsaid),
and what can God know of ignorance,
who cannot feel a single, solitary thing
as we do: as, for a moment, all there is?

Not that he hasn't tried. Once, they tell us,
he let a part of himself be lost
in the dark box of a body, nights like eons
buried alive, the air giving out, each hard breath forever,
so that finally he tore what they call his son
back through the little hole between life and death,
the Earth shuddering, his mother abruptly virgin,
but not before he had cried his one real sentence,
My God, my God, why hast thou forsaken me?
That terrible sentence we hold to, all of us,
in this little room, alone with our wondering
who in the darkness of ourselves we are talking to.

During the Great Storms

After all these years, slow-thoughted trees have understood
that there is a house among them, and troubled
that so swift and wary a creature might escape them,
they have chosen the darkest hour of the loudest storm...
but oh, had they only foreseen the thrill of toppling—
sheer speed, how keen they would feel—if they could have imagined
their unprecedented cry, the long, almost animal
zwwwwisssshhhhh of their sweeping down,
they would long ago have conspired to fall on it
in threes, and slice it like a loaf, lights pouring out!

Watch

Now the wind bends the train horn
around, so that it seems to be coming for me
through the trackless woods.
It is natural, I am told, to wake like this
for two hours in the middle of the night
where there is no one, though it seems
all who have ever talked to the moon can hear.
Ten thousand sorrows, Du Fu? The short way of saying
on such a night ten thousand tributaries
feed the one lake of darkness. On such a night
we could be the same: loose sleeves,
warm cup, the same wars everywhere,
and one page under lamplight
that does not reach to the wall.

As after Sunset Fadeth...

The Adoption

And then when it was almost too late I bent to whisper
It's true what you always suspected. You were not my real parents,
but at a certain age, out of need, and a parent myself,
I chose you freely, this adoption
a secret I have kept from you all these years.
Sleep, it is better this way. It is you I love and mourn,
not the unknown parents I was born to.

Winter Sunsets

All these years my death has gathered
like an evening, taking in
mother and father and brother.
And more and more I speak to no one who answers,
and more and more I dream of nothing that is,
and my thoughts are long, long halls that wander
into this silver darkness: the path, the little pond
only as different from pure dark
as a dark mirror from a dark room.

This is what the dead must see,
and the faint glow on the hills
as after sunset fadeth in the west,
rose-taupe gray-yellow, bronze,
so beautiful as it fails,
so beautiful as I fail
to bring them home,
brother and mother and father.

                              *

This is what the dead must see: their own houses
miles off on dark hills, small as sparks.
One minute dead

and they know they have grown too large and terrible
to go home: earthquake, avalanche.

What is that shudder but the storm of their hands
fumbling at those small doors,

our hearts, that need to be opened
carefully as seeds?

*

Never I carry them, these dead I dream of,
out of my dream
as after sunset fadeth in the west
out of my dream, armfuls of water.

*

As Orpheus among the spirits,
gray flames
throwing up gray arms,
could not be sure of her face.

Why search your memory,
the gods had warned,
for the love that made you, the planet
that holds you? Stand.

But how could he not go down into that story
(he was not sure of her face)
though he saw the end was in the beginning,
that to love her was already to look back?

For My Father

Walking became so hard
I cannot imagine you in ghostly motion,

and since in life you could only take so much of us,
I doubt you wait in the walls to listen.

Probably you keep to yourself, busy and methodical
about whatever it is the dead do,

and even in death have trouble sleeping
(rattle of bottles, flash of refrigerator

waking me). I know you could come back
if you were not embarrassed by your death,

so slow and helpless. It will take years to wash off
our weeks of watching, to forgive our nodding

in hospital chairs, our quick trips home.
I know why you will not speak to me,

but sometimes I call, letting the phone ring
further and further and further into your empty rooms,

until I believe I can see you, yes, maybe dozing,
maybe having a little trouble getting up to answer.

Metamorphosis

The week after you died, Mom,
you were in my checkout line,
little old lady who met my stare
with the fear, the yearning
of a mortal chosen by a god,
feeling herself change
painfully cell by cell
into a shadow, a laurel, you, a constellation.

For My Mother

All I can say,
October's maple
deep and blurred as embers,
reflected, still,
on the moving river.
All I can say, October's
embers of red water.

Refrain

Alas what wind hath torn
the heart's thin curtains...

For you, Mom,
who wanted it all to be as simple
as an old song.

All the Right Tools

*It is aggravating to have to stop writing to fix
things. We hope these tools will get you back to the
important work faster.*

Inscription in a toolbox, a gift from my parents, 1973

That good, slow tool the sun,
with a trumpeter's strict breath,
swells hemispheres of fruits
to scarlet or dusk or amber
imperceptibly,
not breaking one.

That good, slow tool the moon
pulls the quiet
wide-eyed face of the ocean
to its face,
not a drop through its long fingers
slipping down.

That good, slow tool that turns
trees and lives to wreckage
brilliant and strange,
that train so smooth and slow
we hardly know we're on
is Time, but is there one

slower still
that would reverse
these words and call
your breaths and all
your strayed thoughts home
to be you, standing again?

Eye of the Needle

It is easier for a camel to pass through the eye of a needle
than for a rich man to enter into the kingdom of God
>   meaning

you shall not think to carry anything into death,
not luggage under the limit not the slimmest wallet
not the contacts and travel-size cosmetics
that would sail through airport security
>   meaning

it is easier for a camel to pass through the eye of a needle
than to bring into tomorrow
your flash drives and account balances and records of debtors
your résumé your alibis your good deeds
>   meaning

you have brought nothing even into the present
not memory unfogged by the scanners
not backups of your love on the proper medium
not the tedious excuse that ends in who you are
>   meaning

it is easier for a camel to pass through the eye of a needle
easier to see through a star
easier for the eye to see into itself
easier for the right hand to become the left
than to walk out of the shallow water of the page dripping beauty
than to walk out of yourself
to bring anyone where you are or go where anyone is
to see what you have given and know what you have been given
>   meaning

it is stripped from you passing even now through the eye of the needle

That Spring

And suddenly the everywhere tremulous windflowers,
though it was early, so early, barely not snow,
the smallest things I had seen in months, in ever,
fine their white petals, finer—did I even
in all the windless trembling, did I see then,
finer than nerves, their wisps of lavender?
And suddenly why saying why was I saying
Stupid, tearing up, and *Stupid,*
as if I could not would not should not grieve
since I was the one dead, and who,
who now had to go and invent
that stir, that blur in the eye, wind-tender,
that was killing me, that was making me live?

Alternate Routes

Fast Forward

A surge, a lapse, the flicker of a screen,
and every ninety minutes the entire universe
is blanked out and rescanned. Your city is lifted slightly
and resettled, scattering sparrows. Were those clouds
just there, is she really the one
you were talking to?—everything's subtly different,
though when you try to prove it

memories are altered, witnesses conflict,
and since the cosmos, anyway, has a long tradition
of insuperable habit, conservation of energy,
the changes can be undetectably small:
half empty becomes half full, shame
a little less, or more, and just when it seems
you're about to get it... the day reslants,
cutoff calls are sighing in the wires,
old faces alter in new light, new faces
pick up so seamlessly midsentence,
as if they'd always known you,

that maybe you don't even notice,
as I didn't. I'd been time-traveling—in a song, I mean,
that dropped me seven minutes into a future
where something was... how did I get there,
so far underwater on a subway to Brooklyn?
There was a dark woman sitting across from me,
holding her bag tight in her lap, very straight,
brimming, almost taller with trying not not not to,

who swept a tear from her cheek as quickly
as if it were someone else's. I knew she knew

everything, and now, as we surge out onto the plaza,
a bus strains away from the curb, roaring,
and a little crowd of confetti and dust
swirls straight up, as if maybe there's no more gravity,
and something you would have thought was evening,
something cinnamon and cumin, bronzed and sparrowed,
is climbing into the sky for help, and everyone looks up
with something that might be hope, as if they know
it's exactly her thought that's reaching,
reaching across to them, and maybe
we're wrong, and it's a gust, a ghost, a chance, but maybe,
as they have before, as they have so many times before,
the laws of the universe have absolutely changed.

Vectors 4.2: Everyone Else

The power goes off, and the silence wakes me.

*

Take us out of our crowd and we see faces in cliffs, hear voices on the wind, read the thoughts of animals, and feel watched by we don't know what. Unplugged from our peripherals, we're like the newly blind who hallucinate because their brains are desperate to see.

*

Silent or silenced?

*

Spring, and the soil exhales like a pot, lid lifted. The air itself has greened: sound is blurrier and slower, blossoms send out waves of intoxicants. The woodchuck knows exactly how long ago the fox passed, a leaf smells that its neighbor is under attack by insects, from three hundred feet up the hawk spots the tenseness of a vole. No wonder we feel suddenly less and more alone, like someone in a crowd who doesn't know any of the languages.

*

Phone rings. The house has sprung a leak!

*

Silly to have such a strong lock when the door itself is so weak, and the window is weaker, and my head can't keep *anything* out.

*

I'd listen to my conscience if I were sure it was really mine.

*

Her lip's pierced with a ring, last link in some invisible chain.

*

Faith is a kind of doubt... of everything else. And doubt... believes deeply it can do without believing.

*

Zeal: shark that swims hard lest it drown.

*

All that time trying to do what they wanted, when even they weren't quite sure what it was.

*

There's no one less rebellious. Maybe I think I'm in power?

*

My resentment is a child who needs attention. *I'm out of here,* he says. *Don't let me go.*

*

Rage, like infatuation, thrives on silly details.

*

At last I break my chains, only to find that those I was chained to are more relieved than I am.

*

Experience teaches? That the world is just a blaze in my head, pain hurts only me, only others die. The rest is Imagination.

*

They are our friends, or they slump next to us on the subway, or they are close-ups on the News: the sufferers. Next to them, we feel like innocents. Natural enough, but maybe it's analogous to the old sentimentality about *The Happy Poor:* if we envy life's victims for being realer than we are, will we also owe them, will we help them?

*

Some are naked through their clothes, some never naked.

*

Suffering builds character? Or the fear that every touch will be a blow.

*

My pain has to be greater than yours, lest I owe you something.

*

Empathy's the human grid: a voltage surge, and we might shut down so as not to burn out, least responsive to the troubles that are most like our own.

*

Somehow it's easier to believe people are better than I am than that they're smarter.

*

We should be reasonable is a feeling. *Feeling is more genuine than thinking* is a thought.

*

More moving than someone weeping: someone trying not to.

*

On the Kelvin scale, which runs from absolute zero to a zillion degrees, we're most comfortable way down at the chilly end: 293 is room temperature. Only a little higher and water boils, molecules break, life becomes impossible. The universe is a cold place. Good thing!

*

Pain knows you don't really know. Over and over and over it says *No you don't, no you don't!*

*

How messy and wrecked the house has gotten, I think suddenly, and start Spring Cleaning. There must have been a Winter Dirtying I didn't notice, a blindness or lethargy that evolved to protect us from wasting energy during the hard months. But what of those much darker days when, maybe helped by a mirror or a sharp word, I look up from busyness and see how badly I've neglected all that really matters. Surely a different delusion, since it is more likely, after all, in fat times than in lean.

*

Self-criticism: superiority to the idiot I was a minute ago.

*

Evolution provided physical pain to keep us from damaging ourselves, sympathetic pain to keep us from damaging others. Don't feel too good.

*

In heaven we will be known to the core and loved for exactly who we are. Yeah, that's what I was afraid of.

*

Sometimes I'm the only one in the loud bar not talking, a rock in the stream listening for the sound of water hitting it and turning white.

*

Are these new storms, or has everything all together reached the age of falling down?

*

Not till I walk out of the sea of noise into the night do I know I'm drunk.

Big Scenes

And what was King Kong ever going to do
with Fay Wray, or Jessica Lange,
but climb, climb, climb and get shot down?
No wonder Gulliver's amiably chatting
with that six-inch woman in his palm.
Desire's huge, there's really nowhere to put it
in this small world that it will stay put:
might as well just talk.
Rage also, and fear, and elation
are windswept summits, your poor mind
half the time an F6 tornado
that could drive a blade of grass through armor plate.
But a lit match inches from your eyes?
Unwavering.
Out there, in the world called Real, it is calm.
When you stalk down Broadway, fifty feet tall
and building like a thunderhead, your clothes
tattering and whirled away like leaves,
you can nonchalant it, you can be at peace:
it's only in movies that anyone notices.

For Immediate Release

For precious friends hid in death's dateless night

Shakespeare, Sonnet 30

Death is overextended, and tired of the complaints.
He reminds us he routinely takes the easy ones,
the low pale fruit, already half his, since so many
they loved have gone before them that they speak
half the night with ghosts, and winter in his cities.

Somebody has to make the decisions, in the end,
somebody has to say *Enough,* and if you discount
a few brash young, who, if you want to know,
really ask for it (but don't get him going...),
statistically his on-time performance is better than ever,
and if now and then there's some collateral damage,
here and there a beautiful civilian, even a child,
well, in an operation of such size it's to be expected.

It's not so easy being Death, he reminds us.
Who wants him at a wedding, a graduation,
that summer's end impromptu on the patio,
anything short of a war? He has to be satisfied
with doing what he does better than anyone
and bearing alone the burdens of his fame and power,

and even at a stadium, at a park concert, even here
among the billions on Life's Teeming Shore, feeling,
well, conspicuous—you think he hasn't noticed
we lower our voices, look down, change the subject
(defiantly, he's tempted to think). Ah, here he comes,
our old friend Death, in the baggy yellow trunks,

dateless though omnipotent,
even the too-young girls rolling their eyes,
knowing exactly what he has in mind.

Theory of Everything

I pace my little hall, no mystery,
sit by my window listening: birds, of course.
My books, I can hardly read them,
they make so much sense.
Someone skips school. He knows enough.
Someone is fired, there are reasons.
Someone breaks down. There is reason
after reason after reason.
Some patient is cured, and dies of the cure.
Forms are submitted: natural causes.
They rise through the purest offices
like scentless prayers, *We believe.*
Someone's frustration sweeps his desk—
papers fly out. In due course,
they touch the floor, and already
troops move. From the bleeding front
fevers spread, and opportunists like fevers,
as evolution says they must.
Houses are emptied, farms stripped
and Death, chain-smoking commandant,
lights one child off another. Pardon: old story.
What causes are not natural?
Who can object to partly cloudy?
Who disagrees with the news as usual?
You're right, the world has no need for imagination.
It makes sense, it makes so much sense.

My Other Lives

We are all duplicates. None of us are real.

Commander Tuvok

That guy with the rueful smile
and the combination-lock attaché case
that probably smelled like sandwiches, like my dad's,
who I imagined following home
(because he looked like my dad)
now rocks in his boat-size brown recliner
crushing his Diet Coke over and over
in an endless loop—because that's all I imagined.
And that classically beautiful young woman
who turned out to have such a terrible voice?
She's endlessly reliving the three snarky minutes
of what would have been our life together
before we bored each other to death—
because that's all I imagined.

Who knew they actually materialized,
those sad alternate universes
we condemn to existence just by fantasizing—
lives and jobs and loves short-circuited
pffft all lights off, or dragging on like repeating dreams?
I wonder what they have taken with them,
my poor victims, of what was on my mind—
maybe the iris tinge of the rain, that quote
And yet, the ways we miss our lives are life
I was revolving, some sudden face
they'll wonder if they knew or just imagined,
that sense, since who can escape it, of a life
fuller than theirs that they strain to remember.

As for me, what's left of the 1950s
is a yellow tack big as a moon in my bike tire.
The '60s are four or five embarrassments,
as for the '80s, '90s... shouldn't there be
billions of memories?
Count: are there even thousands?

That's how I know. We're someone's glancing thought
of us, in a universe created seconds ago
with the phone in midring, the caller
who thinks he knows why he's calling
that you answer in a voice halting and thick
as if it hadn't yet been used today. The skim of an egg
you don't quite remember making is just
starting to dry, out the window of the kitchen
which has become yours is a scatter of trees
someone forgot to take back, and what's playing is that wisp
of melody I've been searching decades for
through Chopin, Brahms, Scriabin, surer
and surer it's the last eight notes of something
no one has ever heard the beginning of.

Long Stories Short

Quasar

How did the light take forty years
to work its way, through the dancers,
across that crowded room
with a Flash from the early universe:
what your look meant?

What's New?

My heart leaps, running for the stick
you never threw.

Falls

The water's bones, terribly delicate,
break white, heal darkly.

Catch

Bouquets the excited dead
toss from their graves *You next!*

Split

As if when it came time to move on
your furniture had rooted in soft floors,
and posters like morning glories,
having climbed as high as they could, had clung,
and tight-shelved books had blended into one,
and your clothes, drenched so many times
together, could no way be disentangled,
not to mention that
two cells you had lost track of
(a little like the terms of a metaphor)
had interleaved as irreversibly
as two streams flowing together,
wide enough, now, to begin to murmur
your names, her own name.

Uses of Literature

Now I see!
I'm the wicked stepsister,
but here in Life
there is no justice, lucky for me!

Illuminated Manuscript

Maria, moder Godes...
Don't know the family.
But those are utterly
bee, marigold, and fritillary.

Antelope

But language isn't about things, and nouns are the least of it. Probably the first word ever was inseparable from a gesture and a facial expression that went with it, something like *Hey!* When God showed Adam the first of the swift animals, he said *Ah!*, he said *Whoa!*

Wandrers Nachtlied III

This moth and I are loopy
with the perfume,
half lilac and half stone,
of the full moon.

Indispensable

The world
is very small.
Inhale,
and the birds fall.

Noah in Age

It would be the two of us
and two of everything: enough.
We could hardly hear each other
through the clatter of hammers.

Somewhere south, I think,
and with children of her own.
Strangely,
I do not remember any rain.

A Very Small Table

When you wet
your fingertips and pinched
our candle out,
and its twin in the mirror
wavered and
stayed lit...

Vectors 4.3: A Summer Morning

Like a word I've looked up and forgotten.

*

After the shower there's a dry shadow under the maple. Even in this suburban wood there are square inches no one has stepped in since the beginning of time. There are very small spaces time itself has missed.

*

I'm so slow to speak that even silence puts words in my mouth.

*

What was our original sin—disobedience? dishonesty? sex? self-consciousness? The story doesn't care, as long as we remember the part about having to labor to make up for it.

*

I'm not really doing nothing. I'm working not to get in the way of whatever should be doing itself.

*

A tiny pain is like a light in the woods. Hard not to go find out what it is.

*

In their changeless Eden, Adam and Eve could only be tempted by the need to be in a story.

*

Under *boredom,* my dictionary says *origin unknown.*

*

Gods don't read.

*

Sin derives from *es,* the *It is* in a formula something like *It is (true); I did it.* But confession is more than admitting guilt. It is giving up the hope that what you did was uniquely yours and maybe, just maybe, excusable. Others will think they've heard your story before. What you're admitting is that they're right.

*

I guess that was my choice, though what I really wanted was not to choose at all.

*

They revised the Lord's Prayer to *Forgive us our debts as we forgive our debtors,* since we have to believe in what we owe if we want to believe we have something coming to us.

*

You offer help, and suddenly it's more complicated: I have to decide to really do it, and to trouble you, and to owe you.

To be late is to say my time is worth more than yours; to be early, the opposite. But time changes from precious to worthless and back again in no time at all, and we have no idea what we're taking from each other.

*

We say *I have no time,* we hear *I have no time for you.*

*

Left to itself, Time stops, maybe an hour a day—who knows, since you're by definition unaware. Otherwise, it's propelled by crossing things off lists, putting away dollars, tucking vista after vista into tiny cameras. Even as you dispose of one thing, another rushes in to fill the void, and the little wind it makes is Time. In his last years, my father had a tape deck, a video camera, and four VCRs running. Probably he was recording more hours than he actually lived, a Saint of Time, doing it all for the rest of us, bringing on the end.

*

The moment was mine, until I tried to give it to you. Or to keep it for myself, which is the same thing.

*

The moralists told us the vice of age was avarice, but what I saw in my great teachers twenty years later was bitterness that they had not been recognized for what they had done. By now, I feel how deeply *to have* and *to have done* are the same. The résumé is another kind of bank account, and harder to let go of. *Sell all you have,* said a better teacher than any of us.

*

Sad that what's good for the ego is seldom good for the soul.

*

My father, a Depression child, never quite believed in Money. *If you like it, buy two* was his motto, and he turned his salary into Things, their backups, and the tools and spare parts he might need to fix them. He was ready for anything. Predictably, I throw everything away, as if otherwise one day I'd have to pack it all up and take it through airport security. Child of a later era, I am always trying to travel light, clean up, lose weight, forget. But all these words I'm piling up? They are massless, and besides, the books one takes on that plane are not one's own.

*

Let's not burn that bridge till we cross it.

*

At ten, I'm sure I never had the thought *How much of the past I don't remember!* Even at twenty, I assumed it was all down there somewhere, just waiting for the right cue to surface in all its original freshness. Probably my memory was a little sharper then, certainly fewer years were filling it up. But more than that, memory then was spontaneous and passive: it just happened, and the past was whatever I remembered. Now memory is something I actively send back to look for my life, and it returns with unconvincing generalizations—looking out the window, walking to work, Mom.

*

Just on percentages, it's obvious that forgetting is more natural than remembering. And so much of what you remember most vividly serves mainly as a warning against doing again what you're going to want to forget.

*

The self does not exist. But just try to change it.

*

All that reaching for the future: the daydreams, the worry, the waiting, the months I waved away because I just had to finish something. So much of the past has vanished because it was never really the present.

*

I tried. No, to be honest, I tried to try.

*

In the long run there was only the short run.

*

History repeats itself is roughly analogous to *Language repeats itself*. We've heard it all, but we still don't know what's coming next.

*

The books I love best can be read backwards or sideways. Can be read closed, or gazing out a window.

*

Fate? Maybe behind me.

*

My story was that I was past all stories.

*

I try to take it all back, but the tape in reverse is unintelligible.

*

Dear Odysseus. These days, you could fly from Troy to Ithaka in an hour. From 40,000 feet, you could see both at once. Just saying.

*

Time hammers with a feather.

*

Less and less of my life lies before me, but always the whole world.

*

Driving, July: *Bridge May Be Icy.*

Early and Late

Essay on Wood

At dawn when rowboats drum on the dock
and every door in the breathing house bumps softly
as if someone were leaving quietly, I wonder
if something in us is made of wood,
maybe not quite the heart, knocking softly,
or maybe not made of it, but made for its call.

Of all the elements, it is happiest in our houses.
It will sit with us, eat with us, lie down
and hold our books, themselves a rustling woods,
bearing our floors and roofs without weariness,
for unlike us it does not resent its faithfulness
or question *why, for what, how long?*

Its branchings have slowed the invisible feelings of light
into vortices smooth for our hands,
so that every fine-grained handle and page and beam
is a wood-word, a standing wave:
years that never pass, vastness never empty,
speed so great it cannot be told from peace.

Invasive Species

I'd have sworn it was the oldest flower,
midsummer honeysuckle,
whose deep, soft pang was, everywhere,
what even a boy could know about desire.
How strange it is to be learning,
and how late
—and from *Wikipedia,* no less—
it's an *invasive species*
(Japanese), that's classified
noxious in Texas and banned in New Hampshire.

Which brings to mind another ancient friend,
a *dominant understory species,*
which is to say, constituent of shadow,
that crossed the Atlantic on our soles,
so invisibly common
you learn its name, if ever,
long after the names of showier flowers,
or call it by the name for Walking
or all the reliable, unbeautiful Hours
a pretty good day is liable to be made of.

Its real name? Differs in every nation.
And besides, I shouldn't blow its cover,
though it can't be sent home, now its range,
the Americas to Asia,
is roughly that of Indo-European languages.

And today there are the trillion starlings
storming from left to right a full half hour
across our yard, a dark express

descended from an 1890's flock
fanatics released in Central Park
just so Americans could know
all the birds old Shakespeare knew,
a chittery prologue that goes on
and on and on so giddily
that the kids fitting blocks to our patio
shut down their saw and laugh their asses off.

For them, so young, our sixty-odd years,
our thirty-some together,
might as well be forever.
They're Latin, their boss says,
as if they might be the ones
speaking an old, old language.
Cissanthemos, said Pliny—
later, it's *madreselva,*
twinberry, woodbine:
honeysuckle.
Though surely its scent was speechlessly
on the breeze for eons
while ancestors we share with moths
and bees evolved our feeling
that breathing it in is: closing your eyes and falling
up into summer darkness.

Just as *desire* itself,
on something like a wind, has drifted
a long, long way
from *desiderare,* meaning
to want of the stars,
to be with us. The world
is deep, my friend, and older
even than we are.

Let's sit a little:
there's so much we haven't talked about
since talking was invented a minute ago.

It's a strange life. Welcome. Me, I just got here.

Essay on No

The pebble won't open its eyes, posing
roundly but softly its little
no to the light. Better

to be small and dark than concede
more than you should. Yes,
even the satin

yes of a violet is also
a petal by petal, point
by point *maybe*

or maybe not to the lazy
generalization of the air
that *It's all the same.* Shall we call

this reluctance *self,*
or maybe *form?* Vastness
and radiance alone won't cut it—

think of the terrible darkness
the sun is in. Nothing
comes back to it, it can't, for all

its outbound *yesssss* of light,
see or listen (it's the moon,
isn't it,

we tell our troubles to?) *Yes* is
es- , to be. It is what is. God knows
there's more than enough

of that. Even he
feels he's said too much,
remembers fondly his first *No,*

let's wait and see, but now
there's no stopping
the expansion of his universe

from driving into the dark
though there may be
a hairpin turn, a fallen rock,

an oncoming universe
with no headlights, nothing to do
with doubts

but drive faster. Heart knows
there's something about the best
offers that offers

to take itself back. My hand
is thankful for the firm
not mine (your hand) it is surprised

it knew was there, and all
the pleasure in these few
too many words

is feeling them land
in the dark *not that, or anyway*
not only that behind your soft dark eyes.

Fourteen

And if, as the songs say,
there are world-record passions
mine was... but then
I never said her name
to anyone, to her
(I was fourteen).

And if there was a difference
between their *higher and higher*
and some *deeper than the seas*
still to learn,
how could I know?—
I was fourteen

and watching in last period,
as someone making a point
it's taking me decades to get
dipped a long long rose
in liquid nitrogen
and (downbeat) shattered it.

Notes for a Translation of an Ancient Fragment

[She] as the palest curtain
fire behind it
scent of split rock
[She] as the wind
slendered in grass
[She] soft path down which
[Unknown refrain]

As the sea so blue
[a handful, blue]
as the rough blue
[of her eyes, the waves?]
as the cricket [cricket] climbing
nights strong with blue
[Unknown refrain]

As her glass lips say
I shouldn't say this
as her blouse, its slipping
dawn [or down]
Sound [as a verb]
with wide-eyed hands
[Unknown refrain]

As we throw on the fire
live flowers [ourselves]
as the flowers [as limbs]
blend smooth as flames
As the high stars circling will
[how softly, how long?]
shine our bones clean
[Unknown refrain]

Fire Warnings

So much on the verge
of flame.
In a hot
wind anything
is tinder: paper, sage

feverish with bees,
your auburn
hair, my hand
that glows with a thought.
Sunset

or sleepless dawn,
nothing is sure
but what's already burned
water that's ash, steel
that has flowed and cooled,

though in the core
of a star, they too
would fuse and rage,
and even volcanic
glass and char,

and the cold seas,
and even
what we once were
might burn again—
or in the heart.

Vectors 4.4: One or Two Thoughts

Maybe what really interests me in the mirror is not myself but that person who looks so interested in me.

*

Bad dreams as a child I called *night mirrors*.

*

The Me in photographs always looks like he needs help with lines I, too, have forgotten.

*

Man: the animal who is not quite himself.

*

Words that branch from the Indo-European root *dwo*, meaning *two:* twig, twist, twin, twilight, double, doubt.

*

But even words are *beyond words*.

*

The time I least want to see myself is when I'm writing. What genius of hotel design put the mirrors over the desks?

*

I look down, as if just asked for a dollar.

*

Self-deception: how can I not know what I know? I think of someone with a story or excuse that's a little too loud or long, and how it keeps everyone else from talking…

*

Putting on a mask relieves me of the one I was already wearing.

*

I'm not aware of loving myself. But why else would I always be wondering where I am, how I'm doing, what I'm really thinking, what's wrong?

*

The boy who first discovered breasts was hypnotized, stroking their strangely familiar shapeliness as if they had happened to his own body, amazed and amazed that they did not go away.

*

I would never say that. Though I did.

*

When there were more people onscreen than in the seats, we were the ones being watched.

*

Why is it so much easier to cry for the actors—or even for an image in the mirror—than for ourselves?

*

The heart, like the eyes, has a focal length. Very close, you blur. Far off, you might be anyone. It's not so easy to correct near- or far-heartedness—we seek out those with similar distortions of feeling so we can be comfortable at the same distance.

*

After the film, we're stunned that it's dark out, as if we'd walked from one theater into another.

*

De gustibus, I say airily, as if I know whether you see what I see and hate it, or see something completely different.

*

Sometimes it's like we've been standing on line all week. No use talking seriously till we get a table.

*

After a drought, the first drops bounce.

*

By *Love conquers all* they never meant *all obstacles and circum-stances,* only *all people.* Usually it was just the first quick battle with love that was so happily and gratefully lost, over and over. As for really being conquered, from the capital to the backwoods, that could take a long, long time. Even after decades, so many walked away, sadly invincible.

*

Tempting to think that the illumination of our darkest secrets would obliterate us, but chances are someone knows each one of them al-ready. Secrets are secrets *from* someone—your boss, your child, your spouse. They're not a night but a shadow whose shape and depth depends on which way the light is, and how intensely it looks at you.

*

Once only, the wrath of the gods is a Flood. But again and again, two chosen ones drown out the world to start it over.

*

Sometimes tears have risen miles before they brim in the eyes.

*

I've changed sounds way too dramatic and smug. But after all these years of world pouring into me, maybe I'm a little less myself. Or maybe what has really changed is who I think is watching me. Maybe what has changed in me is you.

*

I hear the thunder, I listen to the rain.

*

Our darkest secret is that we don't need each other. Though it's not a secret. Though it's not true.

*

As strange to me as my own hand.

Two Poems I Wish I'd Written

1 *Remember, O Soul*

A little pine tree greens,
who knows where, in the forest,
a rosebush, who can say,
in what garden?
They are already chosen—
remember, O soul!—
to sink roots in your grave
and thrive.

Two black colts grazing
out in a meadow
head home, prancing.
They will step heavily
with your corpse,
maybe, maybe sooner
even than their iron
shoes work loose—
that I see flashing!

Eduard Mörike, "Denk' es, O Seele"

2 *Autumn Day*

Lord: it is time. The summer was immense.
Send your shadow over the sundials
and over the meadows let the winds loose.

Command the last fruits, *Ripen to the core.*
Allow them two more days of summer warmth;
urge them to their fullness, and then drive
the last sweetness into the heavy wine.

Who has no house now: will not build one.
Who is alone now: will be long alone,
will stay up late, and read, and write long letters,
and wander up and down the avenues
restlessly, with the leaves streaming.

Rainer Maria Rilke, "Herbsttag"

End of Fall

Day by day,
the maples in a frenzy letting go
their complications,
I can see deeper
into the woods. All's clearer
and clearer,
then, one moment,
absolutely clear.
Then winter.

Late Aubade

after Hardy

So what do you think, Life, it seemed pretty good to me,
though quiet, I guess, and unspectacular.
It's been so long, I don't know anymore how these things go.
I don't know what it means that we've had this time together.

I get that the coffee, the sunlight on glassware, the Sunday paper
and our studious lightness, not hearing the phone, are iconic
of living regretless in the Now. A Cool that's beyond me:
I'm having some trouble acting suitably poised and ironic.

It's sensible to be calm, not to make too much of a little thing
and just see what happens, as I think you are saying
with your amused look, sipping and letting me monologue,
and young as you are, Life, you would know: you have done it all.

If I get up a little reluctantly, tapping my wallet, keys, tickets,
I'm giving you time to say *Stay, it's a dream*
that you're old—no one notices—years never happened—
but I see you have already given me all that you can.

Those clear eyes are ancient; you've done this with billions of others,
but you are my first life, Life. I feel helplessly young.
I'm a kid checking mail, a kid on his cell with his questions:
are we in love, Life, are we exclusive, are we forever?

Essay on Clouds

Maybe a whale, as Hamlet mused,
or a camel or weasel,
more likely a hill, still likelier

a school of hills, since (as with us)
true singletons are rare.
We compare them mostly

to silent things, sensing
that thunder is something else
that gets into them—a stone, a god—

and as for what they want to say,
aeromancy, which presumed to interpret,
never caught on. After all,

clouds weren't reliable predictors
even of rain, and if they had a message
for us, we guessed,

it would hardly be practical:
clouds are not about
about, showing instead

boundless detail without specificity.
Whales, sure (which might in turn be
blue clouds), but we don't say

How very like a screwdriver,
or *my house,* or *my uncle,* or certainly
how unlike my uncle. For though a blend

of winds we don't at our level
necessarily feel lends them
amazing motion, that's not the same as

intention, so failure
is not in question. We wouldn't say
That cloud is derivative, jejune,

disproportionate, strained, misplaced
or (since they affirm nothing)
That cloud is wrong,

though truly they often bear down
on exactly the wrong moment—that overcast,
is it one cloud or ten thousand

that makes everything feel so gray
forever? From inside, of course—think
of flying through one—

a cloud has no shape. As with us: only
when someone looks hard, or we catch
our reflections, do we solidify as

whale
weasel
fool

and plummet. Though large clouds weigh
more than a 747, not one
has ever crashed, so admirably

do they spread their weight, a gift
it is not too much to hope
we could possess, since according to Porchia

we *are* clouds: *If I were stone*
and not cloud, my thoughts,
which are wind, would abandon me. O

miracle not miraculous! Everything
we know well
lightens and escapes us, and isn't that

when *we* escape? So just as
Old and Middle English *clūd*
meant *rock* or *hill,* but now

means *cloud,* really I mean
in exactly the same way that stone
got over being stone

and rose, we rise.

Very Late

Even our tenderest
buds and shoots
(though we are pained)
endure unharmed
the late, late snow,
which is, as cold goes,
almost warm.

During. I like prepositions, even without objects. And this one shares roots with *durable, endure, duration, duress.*

"Again." The Titan Mnemosyne, personification of Memory, was the mother of the nine Muses. This poem is for Connie, who knows why.

"Essay Traversed by Deer." Actaeon stumbled upon Artemis and her nymphs bathing, and she turned him into a stag. The dressing of deer carcasses is described vividly and at length in part III of *Sir Gawain and the Green Knight.*

"Solo." On June 25, 1961, at the Village Vanguard, the Bill Evans Trio (Evans, Scott LaFaro, and Paul Motian) recorded the material for *Sunday at the Village Vanguard* and *Waltz for Debby,* which includes two takes of "Detour Ahead." A landmark recording? No clue; it's just one I find particularly beautiful. Please feel free to substitute your own song.

"Sentence." "My God, my God, why hast thou forsaken me." Jesus said it on the Cross.

"Watch." Just FYI, "Until the close of the early modern era, Western Europeans on most evenings experienced two major intervals of sleep bridged by up to an hour or more of quiet wakefulness." "First sleep" was followed by what was sometimes called "watch" or "watching," and then "second" or "morning" sleep. A. Roger Ekirch, *At Day's Close: Night in Times Past.*

"Winter Sunsets." "As after sunset fadeth in the west" is line six of Shakespeare's touchstone Sonnet 73. Later on, it's Orpheus and Eurydice, as I probably don't need to say.

"Eye of the Needle." "It is easier for a camel to pass through the eye of a needle than for a rich man to enter into the kingdom of God." Jesus says it in three of the Gospels.

"Fast Forward." If you're old enough to wake and see the clock every ninety minutes, you'll know the significance of this number in the sleep/wake cycle. I've had the thought that it's also the length of a mood.

"My Other Lives." This poem is for Whitney Terrell. Commander Tuvok, in the best episode of *Star Trek: Voyager.* "And yet, the ways we miss our lives are life": this All-Time Top Ten line is from Randall Jarrell's "A Girl in a Library."

"Quasar." Quasars are extremely luminous galactic nuclei. They are billions of light-years away, i.e., their light has taken billions of years to reach us.

"Illuminated Manuscript." Maybe this one's still exhibited at the Getty. "Mary, mother of God."

"Invasive Species." All the stuff about honeysuckle, starlings, and the unnamed white flower (which I'm not ratting out here) can be verified in *Wikipedia,* trust me. Indo-European: family that includes most languages spoken in a band from Ireland to India, including Latin, Spanish, and English. *Desire* comes from Latin *desiderare,* which itself comes from *sidus, sideris = star,* which can also be heard in *sidereal* and *consider,* literally "[to consult] with the stars."

"Two Poems I Wish I'd Written." I met these two as a teenager failing to learn German and have been in love ever since. The originals are:

Denk' es, O Seele!

Ein Tännlein grünet, wo,
Wer weiß! im Walde,
Ein Rosenstrauch, wer sagt,
In welchem Garten?
Sie sind erlesen schon,
Denk' es, o Seele,
Auf deinem Grab zu wurzeln
Und zu wachsen.

Zwei schwarze Rößlein weiden
Auf der Wiese,
Sie kehren heim zur Stadt
In muntren Sprüngen.
Sie werden schrittweis gehn
Mit deiner Leiche;
Vielleicht, vielleicht noch eh'
An ihren Hufen
Das Eisen los wird,
Das ich blitzen sehe!

Eduard Mörike (1804–1875)

Herbsttag

Herr: es ist Zeit. Der Sommer war sehr groß.
Leg deinen Schatten auf die Sonnenuhren,
und auf den Fluren laß die Winde los.

Befiel den letzten Früchten voll zu sein;
gib ihnen noch zwei südlichere Tage,
dränge sie zur Vollendung hin und jage
die letzte Süße in den schweren Wein.

Wer jetzt kein Haus hat, baut sich keines mehr.
Wer jetzt allein ist, wird Es lange bleiben,
wird wachen, lesen, lange Briefe schreiben
und wird in den Alleen hin und her
unruhig wandern, wenn die Blätter treiben.

Rainer Maria Rilke (1875–1926)

"Late Aubade." An aubade is a dawn song, for the parting of lovers. A "late aubade" would be faintly paradoxical. Thomas Hardy published his first book of poems in his late fifties, some of his best in his seventies and eighties. Not surprisingly, he had a habit of writing Farewells to Life. Mine reminds me a little of "He Never Expected Much."

"Essay on Clouds." "If I were stone…" is a reasonable translation of Antonio Porchia's *"Si yo fuese como una roca y no como una nube, mi pensar, que es como el viento, me abandonaría."* His *Voces Abandonadas* is one of the Great Books, probably the Greatest, if you're talking aphorisms. See W.S. Merwin's terrific English versions in *Voices*.

James Richardson's most recent books are *By the Numbers: Poems and Aphorisms,* which was a *Publishers Weekly* "Best Book of 2010" and a finalist for the National Book Award; *Interglacial: New and Selected Poems & Aphorisms,* a finalist for the National Book Critics Circle Award; and *Vectors: Aphorisms and Ten-Second Essays.* His work appears in *The New Yorker, The Nation, T: The New York Times Style Magazine, Narrative, Yale Review, Copper Nickel, Great American Prose Poems, Geary's Guide to the World's Great Aphorists,* and several numbers of *The Best American Poetry* series and the Pushcart Prize anthology. Winner of the Jackson Poetry Prize, an Award in Literature from the American Academy of Arts and Letters, and fellowships from the National Endowment for the Arts, the National Endowment for the Humanities, and the New Jersey State Council for the Arts, he is professor of creative writing at Princeton University. He lives in New Jersey with his wife, the scholar and critic Constance W. Hassett.

Poetry is vital to language and living. Since 1972, Copper Canyon Press has published extraordinary poetry from around the world to engage the imaginations and intellects of readers, writers, booksellers, librarians, teachers, students, and donors.

WE ARE GRATEFUL FOR THE MAJOR SUPPORT PROVIDED BY:

THE PAUL G. ALLEN FAMILY FOUNDATION

 CULTURE

Lannan

ART WORKS. National Endowment for the Arts arts.gov

OFFICE OF ARTS & CULTURE
SEATTLE

 WASHINGTON STATE ARTS COMMISSION

Anonymous

John Branch

Diana Broze

Beroz Ferrell & The Point, LLC

Janet and Les Cox

Mimi Gardner Gates

Linda Gerrard and Walter Parsons

Gull Industries, Inc.
on behalf of William and
Ruth True

Mark Hamilton and Suzie Rapp

Carolyn and Robert Hedin

Steven Myron Holl

Lakeside Industries, Inc.
on behalf of Jeanne Marie Lee

Maureen Lee and Mark Busto

Brice Marden

Ellie Mathews and Carl Youngmann
as The North Press

H. Stewart Parker

Penny and Jerry Peabody

John Phillips and Anne O'Donnell

Joseph C. Roberts

Cynthia Lovelace Sears and
Frank Buxton

The Seattle Foundation

Kim and Jeff Seely

David and Catherine Eaton Skinner

Dan Waggoner

C.D. Wright and Forrest Gander

Charles and Barbara Wright

The dedicated interns and faithful volunteers of Copper Canyon Press

TO LEARN MORE ABOUT UNDERWRITING COPPER CANYON PRESS TITLES,
PLEASE CALL 360-385-4925 EXT. 103

诗

The Chinese character for poetry is made up of two parts:
"word" and "temple." It also serves as pressmark for
Copper Canyon Press.

The poems are set in Sabon.
Printed on archival-quality paper.
Book design and composition by Phil Kovacevich.

31901059347122